"But be very careful to keep the commandment and the law that Moses the servant of the LORD gave you: to love the LORD your God, to walk in obedience to him, to keep his commands, to hold fast to him and to serve him with all your heart and with all your soul."

Joshua 22,5

Our Father ... for Thine is...
The spiritual way in Christ

1st edition 2022
by Andrea Regina Katharina InEssenz
www.andrea-inessenz.de
(Original Title: VaterUnser ... denn Dein ist ...
Der geistige Weg in CRISTUS)
Translated from German by Vincenzo Benestante

Editor / Authoress: Andrea InEssenz
Cover design, typesetting & layout: Roland H-P Lutz
ISBN 978 3 949324 17 8 (Paperback)

Credit:
Cover picture: Fabijenna D. Wagner
S. 1, S- 12, S. 22, S. 73 & Rückumschlag: Roland H-P Lutz
S. 6 Pexals / S. 14 & 32 Gerd Altmann / S. 42 Barbara Jackson / S. 48 S.Hermann & F.Richter / S. 56 jplenio / S. 64 Jan Alexander / S. 71 JF: all Pixabay

On the author's website you will find more current, especially mystical texts. Visit for this:
www.andrea-inessenz.de or follow her on:
facebook: / Andreainessenz vimeo: / andreainessenz
youtube: // Andrea InEssenz

Our Father

... for Thine is ...

The spiritual way in **CHRIST**

edition inessenz

Preface

About Prayer. Our Father.

"And when you pray, do not be like the hypocrites, for they love to pray standing in the synagogues and on the street corners to be seen by others. Truly I tell you, they have received their reward in full.

But when you pray, go into your room, close the door and pray to your Father, who is unseen. Then your Father, who sees what is done in secret, will reward you.

And when you pray, do not keep on babbling like pagans, for they think they will be heard because of their many words.

Do not be like them, for your Father knows what you need before you ask him.

"This, then, is how you should pray: "

'Our Father in heaven!
Hallowed be your name,

Your kingdom come. Your will be done, on earth as it is in heaven.

Give us today our daily bread.

And forgive us our debts, as we also have forgiven our debtors.

And lead us not into temptation, but deliver us from the evil one. (For Thine is the Kingdom and the power and the glory, forever and ever. Amen)'

For if you forgive other people when they sin against you, your heavenly Father will also forgive you.

But if you do not forgive others their sins, your Father will not forgive your sins."

Matthew 6, 5-15

Chapter 1
The Lord's Prayer

You are our Father

On a seemingly endless quest – for at least 6000 years – man has searched for the sense of his existence. He lives, dies, is born, and dies once again. In all human experience, the loss of truth lies at the roots. The truth is found with God the Father in heaven; the actual home of the soul.

At the beginning of its long journey through the spiritual realm, the soul was given a secure bond which connected it to its home. The Father gave the soul the spirit of worship. Through this gift we can pray and be spiritually nourished by emanations of home. **When we pray frequently, we are "well-fed" and at peace.**

The one prayer which truly connects the soul to God, who is our Father, is the Lord's Prayer.

This is essentially God's commitment, "I am your Father" and the soul confirms this through prayer: "Hallowed be Thy name."

When Jesus, the Son of God, came to us, he reminded us of this prayer; because we had forgotten it and thus, our souls were spiritually impoverished.

Jesus himself taught us this prayer by which we could speak to the Father. He urged us to be staunch and intimate while praying, so that we could truly understand and experience the meaning and the consequences of these words.

Christians the world over are familiar with the Lord's Prayer and it probably binds all the diverse Christian groups together as the sole fertile soil of all Christian beliefs.

Many people, however, recite this wonderful prayer out of sheer habit and with empty hearts. Whoever does not really live the love for the Father, for God, can certainly articulate this prayer, but then it is nothing but a collection of empty words without spiritual significance.

Why this prayer is so important

God created the soul and brought it into existence through Christ. It is his child and therefore God is its Father.

The assignment of the soul here in the world of visible creation is to complete a process of development. The soul must let God come alive within itself and distribute the fruits of his love in this world, which is overshadowed by sin.

The world into which the soul is sent as a living human soul, is transformed into a world of intellect through the workings of the shadow.

The knowledge, which comes from the mind and seeps into the soul, does not turn towards God, but instead draws it away from the Father and binds it to the shadow.

When the Bible speaks of living a "spiritual relationship" with God

"Yet to all who did receive him, to those who believed in his name, he gave the right to become children of God - children born not of natural descent, nor of human decision or a husband's will, but born of God."

John 1, 12-13

this means nothing other than:

"Jesus answered: Verily I say unto you, no one can enter into the kingdom of God unless they are born of water and spirit."

John 3,5

The progress of the soul is made possible through the prayer, which Jesus brought into the world - the Our Father. The soul turns to God and returns thereby to the "House of the Father".

If this prayer, however, is merely recited as lip service, and a person simply rattles it off, it achieves nothing within the soul. All that remains is an empty word without meaning.

Let's look into the spirit of this prayer together and let it become alive in our souls.

Jesus is the spirit of The Lord's Prayer

"I am the way and the truth and the life. No one comes to the Father except through me."

John 14,6

Whoever does not know or does not accept Jesus Christ, the Son of God, can neither understand the Lord's Prayer, nor experience it. He/she can recite it by rote within the realm of the intellectual and external world; he/she can use it as a prayer, but it will be void of spiritual abundance.

Jesus Christ is the spirit, which lifts up the soul to God. We find seven steps in prayer. Every single one of them carries its own spiritual direction – a promise; a supportive strength, which leads towards a certain goal. The soul is refined within God; therefore, the seven steps.

Prayer is based upon godly order and therefore has as its purpose – **the opening of the soul to godly love.**

The first step

Our Father

These two words of the Lord's Prayer are already completely sufficient. Whoever wishes to follow religion can accept these words as the one, absolute truth.

In themselves they are religion and confirm its very spirit. They require in this; the first step; nothing other than themselves.

"Our Father" is the affirmation in and of God. Here God states: "Yes, it is I," and His child - the soul - responds with "Yes, it is You".

Speaking this dialogue is synonymous with love! The Father and the child are united through them.

If we observe this world, we all know that - as children - we need a father, who guides and loves us; whom we trust; who supports us, teaches us; and much more. We are also aware that we cannot always have such a father on this earthly journey. It is therefore all the more a blessing, that we all

- regardless of who we are - have been granted this same Father, who compensates for all imperfect fathers. Jesus said:
"If you, then, who are evil, know how to give good gifts to your children, how much more will your Father in heaven give the Holy Spirit to those who ask him?"

Luke 11,13

These words demonstrate how God is the perfect father and gives us all that we need for the development of our souls.

Our Father - God is our Father and we are his children; we are descendants of his spirit and therefore we are similar to the essence of God.

Which inheritance was given to us? We are a spiritual thought of God and if we turn to him, the fruits of his spirit bloom within us. Jesus came to mankind, in order to bring this inheritance closer to us. He came in order to give himself as the way which leads our souls home to the Father.

Here - right here - we can recognise that if we have come from God, then our souls are his children. Therefore, we are images of God, created by the one creative spirit; through the holy breath, which he breathed into us. And so the children of God were created.

At this point all theologians can withdraw all their theories about God. A wonderful "product" has come to being through God. He expressed himself; his spirit wandered through all of his realms and entered the realm of darkness. The soul is the tool for this purpose - its function is to render God visible.

Everything finds sustenance here - "Our Father" is love!

A spiritual connection to God is synonymous with the welfare of the human being. Our souls are thereby healthy and free from the burden of the shadows, which had grasped them.

Our Father - these two words, brought to us by Jesus, also tell us: **We are all brothers and sisters.** We have one Father.

Thus, Jesus gives us a unified spirit - as well as the right for all of us to claim this one Father.

In this world which we have formed, there are many opinions about God. Some people believe God belongs to them because they call themselves Christians. And yet, even Hindus, Buddhists, Moslems, all sexes and all self-proclaimed religions and groups have one father. **It is not my Father, to whom we pray, it is OUR FATHER.**

"See what great love the Father has lavished on us, that we should be called the children of God! And that is what we are! The reason that the world does not know us is that it did not know him."

1 John 3,1

The second step

Who art in heaven

Jesus has now said – crystal clear and fully certain – that when you pray, pray to our common Father. All of us; and Jesus, the Son of God, have one and the same Papa. However, the Son also tells us where this Father resides – namely, in heaven.

Heaven means the exalted, the pure, the absolute. Heaven is the house of God – a residence of unconditional love. Here act only the spirit of God and the spirits of those who are the pure, spiritual messengers of God. Dark evil has no right to exist here. Everything created here is exclusively good, as God, too, is good.

Heaven is full of dwellings. These are spiritual premises, in which souls have their homes. Here they create with and for God a spiritual space for eternal life in the love of God. Heaven is not a place which can be described in human terms. Believing that God and heaven together are the goal of our eternal existence should be sufficient for us all.

"And I heard a loud voice from the throne saying, "Look! God's dwelling place is now among the people and he will dwell with them. They will be his people, and God himself will be with them and be their God. He will wipe every tear from their eyes. There will be no more death or mourning or crying or pain, for the old order of things has passed away."

Revelations 21,3-4

"Our Father, who art in heaven," lets us recognise that we have a Father, who is in heaven, and that we are still on Earth. Whoever wants to live in heaven must go to the Father; because he is the creator. Through his presence in us, our souls can return home.

Jesus, who came to us, brought this prayer as a living spirit to us all. With that, he made us understand that we are still separated from true glory - and that God waits for us. This prayer leads us back into the arms of the Father and conquers the realm of shadows.

"My Father's house has many rooms; if that were not so, would I have told you that I am going there

to prepare a place for you? And if I go and prepare a place for you, I will come back and take you to be with me that you also may be where I am."

John 14,2-3

Jesus is the way. He leads us all to the Father, our God in heaven. This spiritual location is described many times in the bible. As a written word, "heaven" is little more than a tiny hint of its true, perfect beauty.

"The wolf and the lamb will feed together, and the lion will eat straw like the ox, and dust will be the serpent's food. They will neither harm nor destroy on all my holy mountain, says the LORD."

Isaiah 65,25

"Then will the eyes of the blind be opened and the ears of the deaf unstopped. Then will the lame leap like a deer and the mute tongue shout for joy. Water will gush forth in the wilderness and streams in the desert."

Isaiah 35,5-6

**"For you created my inmost being;
you knit me together in my
mother's womb.**

**I praise you because I am fearfully
and wonderfully made;
your works are wonderful,
I know that full well."**

Psalms 139,13-14

The third step

Hallowed be thy name

"But when you pray, go into your room, close the door and pray to your Father, who is unseen. Then your Father, who sees what is done in secret, will reward you.

And when you pray, do not keep on babbling like pagans, for they think they will be heard because of their many words. Do not be like them, for your Father knows what you need before you ask him.

This, then, is how you should pray: 'Our Father in heaven, hallowed be your name'."

Matthew 6,6-9

We all know deep within, that God is the absolute, the true and the good.

All that comes out of our thoughts, mouths and deeds should be exactly as good. When we glorify the name of God, we are then the fruits of his spirit.

"Father, glorify your name!" Then a voice came from heaven, "I have glorified it, and will glorify it again."

John 12,28

The name of God is simultaneously his nature. The origin of the word "hallowed", is healing, or destined to heal. When we recognise and experience God as "hallowed", he is not only worthy of worship; no, he is absolute, perfect and without flaw.

The soul - in its pure spiritual form - worships God in exactly this way. It hallows him and desires to be in his presence. It causes the soul immense pain to be separated from God and to be alienated from his holiness. It is absolutely clear for us: **Without God there can be no good.**

"Therefore, I urge you, brothers and sisters, in view of God's mercy, to offer your bodies as a living sacrifice, holy and pleasing to God - this is your true and proper worship."

Romans 12,1

The fourth step

Thy kingdom come, thy will be done, on Earth as it is in heaven

This phrase from the Lord's Prayer is our request to God, to grant his salvation to all of mankind. Jesus brings his followers to understand that - in the times to come, when God himself will rule the world in love - **there will be no more war, no injustice and no hunger; as soon as God's will is done.**

Let us examine the nature of the prayer.
Everything is focussed on God:

- Hallowed be THY name.
- THY kingdom come.
- THY will be done.

We petition God to fill us with his spirit. Thereby the Name of God is sanctified. Here the urgency of the soul, which underlies this prayer to God, is revealed. It is not about "asking for a gift". Rather, this concerns the fulfilment of the soul's spirit through the spirit of God. By this means, a person will become a good, living image; and he/she will fulfil the legacy of Jesus, who has exemplified this for us all. His way of life here in this world was one, single eulogy to his PAPA in heaven - and he said to us; God is not only his Father; **he is the Father of us all.**

What we all pray today, Jesus lived.

As Jesus was on the verge of his death on the cross, he implored the Father, let this cup pass me by. However, he also spoke out what stands on the fourth step of the prayer: **let not my will be done, but thy will be done.**

With that Jesus interrupts Satan's influence in his life. He interrupts the violence which was performed on him. Although this extreme violence was carried out, the spirit of God descended into Jesus nonetheless. Consequently it reached out and touched all the people who had taken part in the event.

The reader probably needs a moment to be able to understand what is meant by this.

Jesus was condemned unfairly and crucifixion awaited him. However, he does not assume the role of the victim, nor does he become a perpetrator full of lust for revenge. He leaves the spirit of blood vengeance entirely: "an eye for an eye, a tooth for a tooth."

Jesus accepts God's will. He makes peace with his betrayers, his torturers, and with his death. Thus the crucifixion loses its "bitter taste". Instead, we glean a foretaste of heaven, where love soothes all pain.

Jesus, the Son of God, is the way to heaven for us.

His death showed us how to forgive the greatest injustice. This is solely possible through God as our Father.

Nevertheless, we humans are often unable to accept God's will, because one thing is certain: this cannot be recognised through intellect. Only love for God and our commitment allow us to accept the incomprehensible. This is the art and secret of true faith.

"And without faith it is impossible to please God, because anyone who comes to him must believe that he exists and that he rewards those who earnestly seek him."

Hebrews 11,6

The fifth step

Give us this day our daily bread

"Then Jesus was led by the Spirit into the wilderness to be tempted by the devil.
After fasting forty days and forty nights, he was hungry.
The tempter came to him and said, 'If you are the Son of God, tell these stones to become bread.'
Jesus answered, "It is written (5 Moses 8,3): 'Man shall not live on bread alone, but on every word that comes from the mouth of God.'"

Matthew 4,1-4

We all wish to be cared for and to be nurtured. Our earthly parents should fulfil our wishes. Not only physically, but rather, generally speaking, for a full, rich life. They are our providers, when we are children.

As adults we are still these children. Our needs of happiness, peace and satiety are the same as in our beginning. However, our mothers and fathers no longer carry the responsibility of fulfilling these needs for us.

Now we are mostly reminded of our invisible Father - God in heaven. Many people turn to him, in order that he may fulfil their desires. "Give us this day our daily bread", thus represents a wish; even a requirement.

It's without question that God wants us to have everything which puts our minds and bodies at rest and frees us from shortages and other grievances. It is God's explicit wish, that this be so.

Should a person lead a deficient life in many areas of existence, it is obvious that he/she will look for other sources to fulfil his/her requirements. Because what God gives, alleviates hunger and any other deficiencies.

However, if we look to humans and concrete things for the fulfilment of our bodily and mental sustenance, we programme our minds to the material. Thereby our souls suffer endless torture and literally starve. Souls live solely through the presence of God. Through Jesus Christ, who came to us as the word made flesh, we have received our daily bread; for we satiate our bodies and souls through experience, which leads to insight.

If we believe in God, but remain without insight, we remain hungry and thirsty. In every experience lies a higher spiritual meaning. If a situation brings us to our limits, it requires us to be insightful. Only then will a further spiritual gate be opened and our situation will become clear and understandable.

If we wish to convert experience into insight, we must pray vitally. This implies not merely believing superficially in our provider in heaven, but rather to experience our lives and all of our situations together with God. This is the bread which we then receive. Through his living presence within us, we make our souls rich and give them the freedom which God has granted them. Our daily bread comes from God alone; and Jesus Christ makes it tangible for us, if we go with him together to the Father.

The sixth step

And forgive us our trespasses, as we forgive those who trespass against us

This phrase is a turning point, a return; turning back. Jesus brought us the Lord's Prayer. With this he gave us in just a few sentences all the essentials we need in order for our souls to develop into their full potential in the presence of God.

In this prayer, everything which brings us salvation is brought to a point. No explanations or word games are introduced here. These seven steps reach our souls in detail. If we adjust our characters unswervingly to these directives, our souls can fee themselves completely from the presence of Satan.

Our prayers, our dialogues, which we execute with God or Jesus, all carry a liberating strength in themselves, but solely the Lord's Prayer leads the way to our eternal home.

The forgiveness of all sins is the only true assignment of human nature. We all live through the volition of God. HE WANTED US ALL. We are his creation, brought forth through the spirit of Christ. He makes all of existence appear.

- We are only on this Earth due to sin
- Only because of sin is this world such as it is
- Only because of sin do we suffer intrinsically and at the hands of others.

Sin is a feeling of being unapproachable and bears the greatest human tragedy. Its very nature contains selfishness and the illusion of being independently valuable in this world. Sin wants to own and can therefore only bring about - and follow - desire and longing. In this obsession with acknowledgment, the actual truth of human nature is lost. Sin forces God out of the soul and establishes its own character in the human personality.

However, our true spiritual ego is one with God. It expresses the character of God and brings its will into the world. Hence it embodies godly characteristics. The graces of spiritual nature bear witness to the presence of God in us.

"For in him we live and move and have our being. As some of your own poets have said, 'We are his offspring'. Therefore, since we are God's offspring, we should not think that the divine being is like gold or silver or stone - an image made by man's design and skill."

Acts 17,28

The spirit of sin, however, has only one thing in mind: it wants to negate our thoughts of God.

If we observe this world and ourselves, we clearly recognise what the enemy of God has in mind. He wants to bring us to believe, that we are all-powerful and can master ourselves and our characters.

If we believe that to be our truth, we will continue to experience competition, strife, misery and sorrow of all types and intensity. We will be living in sin. It has become our daily routine; it was programmed into our minds. The temptation of sin has established itself within us. This spiritual programme is exclusively self-destructive and would - if it remained - condition us all spiritually, mentally and physically to mortality without life thereafter. Were it not for the spirit of forgiveness, terrible things would happen to us all.

Jesus tells us clearly through the Lord's Prayer:

No person has the right to freedom and forgiveness, if he/she does not first forgive him-/herself, as well as all brothers and sisters. There is no room for bargaining here.

Nobody can ask God: "Father, forgive my sins. I'll try to forgive others who have wronged me someday." No, our freedom depends solely on how we forgive others. Otherwise, this amounts to reciting a prayer without belief. In that case, of course, we would not receive. It's exactly the same with forgiveness. We receive no forgiveness from God if we remain resentful or unforgiving.

But first - before any other forgiveness - stands self-forgiveness. If we cannot forgive ourselves, we are not able to grant forgiveness to others. We remain trapped in our self-authority: and that is like being on a carousel: everything revolves around itself.

If we wish to truly forgive ourselves and others, we must first give our lives over to Jesus.*

He shall make the Our Father come to life within our soul, step by step.

Lead us not into temptation (or: lead us through temptation), but deliver us from evil.

This request to God has been controversial throughout the ages. Many people say that Jesus never stated this in the Lord's Prayer, because God never wanted to lead us into temptation. But Jesus meant it so, for we can change the expression to "Lead us through temptation." However, the original request can easily be explained here.

This prayer should bring liberation to the soul; provided we are truly perceptive of the prayer. We must pray earnestly and put into practice that which it contains. It is a compass, which leads outward from sin and ends in the deliverance from all transgressions and their consequences. The soul

**see "The Prayer of commitment to Jesus" on page 113 in the book "The Seven world Demons and Salvation through JESUS The CHRIST" by Andrea InEssenz* descended through the so-called spiritual veil of sin. Due to this, the original sin-spirit streamed into it and with its first breath of life, the soul gave birth to the legacy succession of sinfulness.

Each of us experiences earthly life in a different manner. The individual traits create countless character features. These contribute to shape the essence of our personalities and therefore also the nature of our souls. If a soul becomes bound to temptation and its facades, then the person is separated from God and will suffer. Jesus knew that when we enter into the world, we - and our souls - would encounter darkness, for it was incarnated with the flesh and soul as well.

When "Lead us NOT into temptation," is spoken in the Lord's Prayer, it means, "Dear God, spare me from temptations, which I cannot recognise, nor subdue; but should it occur nonetheless, then redeem me from this evil."

That is the meaning of this wording. God, of course, would never willingly lead us into temptation, yet he must allow it to come, for it is our mission to recognise and resist it. In this vein, we can accept this phrase, which Jesus spoke, as it stands.

Some souls arrive daringly. They seek horrible experiences in order to evolve quickly. In so doing, they omit God's intended method of spiritual growth, which should happen gradually. They challenge God, so to speak, to lead them into temptation. Jesus, who sees through all souls, recognised this and gave them the assurance, not to let them fall into temptation. Thus can this phrase be understood correctly.

The version, "Lead us through temptation," can be prayed additionally, in order to tell God, "Father in heaven, stay with me in all things and save me from the evil in and around me."

Thus, be consoled, for this prayer is word for word the salvation of your soul.

The seventh step

For thine is the kingdom and the power and the glory forever and ever. Amen

This sentence is an affirmation, a declaration of love to God.

It states:

- Father, you are everything
- All of creation belongs to you
- Heaven is yours
- The Earth is yours
- I am yours
- So be it for all eternity

Whoever prays this sentence (For thine is the kingdom ...) and means it sincerely, binds him/herself to God and is in a wonderful fellowship with him. This person says yes to God, of his/her own volition and even allows him/herself to be dependent on God. For the entire Lord's Prayer demonstrates how much we need his grace, his love, his beauty, his very being. **Without HIM we do not exist.**

His breath fills our lungs. Our bodies vibrate through his spirit in a living tone. His thoughts have created all that we see in nature. All life stems from his will.

Christ, the eternal spirit, which brought forth the Son, made all of existence visible. All souls became eternal light through him.

The Holy Spirit permeates this existence and connects everything to God.

Thus do we praise and extol him, the Father, the Son, and the Holy Spirit. Through our lives we give ourselves to Jesus. He showed us all by his own example, how we could honour God, how we could live in health and become love personified – **through the avowal OUR Father ...**

Chapter 2
Mental and spiritual transformation

Why is Mankind without peace?

Humankind has tried to find inner peace, to experience healing and to live in ease and joy for as long as it has existed.

The separation from God, from the paradisiacal state of being, has CONSEQUENCES!

There is a primordial form; an original cause, which is responsible for how we live and experience now: the so-called first disobedience of Adam and Eve. God gave them a directive, as to how they were to comport themselves in paradise according to his rightful will. Eve, however, cast it to the wind and followed instead the voice (serpent) of God's great adversary, the devil!

Thus, she interrupted the original trust to her creator and the righteous communion with him. She followed the original power of evil and temptation. This is the original catastrophe, which is the root of all catastrophes; collectively and individually. All forms of misery and suffering stem from this original offence. They all accompany mankind, who wished "to be like GOD".

We all are descendants of Adam, and therefore, we live under the influence of the evil in this world. He, the devil, hates God above all things and uses men as tools, to weaken God and to take possession of his creation. Mankind shouldn't wonder that this earth is permeated by misery and catastrophes, wars, inhuman deeds like rape and murder, hunger and many schisms and heresies - they all stem from the lack of a close relationship with God. Here, corruption and fraud reign. Evil hypnotizes man's spirit and drags it down, far away from love and peace.

What can Man do for God?

Through Jesus, God has given us righteous so-called laws, which in fact represent a caring guide.

God gave us clear instructions in his word as to how we are to live for him. These include loving one another, the call to follow him - even at the expense of our own wishes - the exhortation to care for the poor and suffering; and the warning not to fall into sinful behaviour, as do those who do not know him.

Jesus summarised a life for God, when a teacher of the law asked him about the most important commandment. *"The most important one," answered Jesus, "is this: 'Hear, O Israel: The Lord our God, the Lord is one. Love the Lord your God with all your heart and with all your soul and with all your mind and with all your strength.' The second is this: 'Love your neighbour as yourself.' There is no commandment greater than these."*

Mark 12,29-31

Jesus' prayer before the crucifixion also enlightens us as to the meaning of life. Regarding believers, he prayed: *"I have given them the glory that you gave me, that they may be one as we are one - I in them and you in me - so that they may be brought to complete unity. Then the world will know that you sent me and have loved them even as you have loved me. Father, I want those you have given me to be with me where I am, and to see my glory, the glory you have given me because you loved me before the creation of the world. Righteous Father, though the world does not know you, I know you, and they know that you have sent me. And I have made you known to them, and I will continue to make you known, in order that the love you have for me may be in them and that I myself may be in them."*

John 17,22-26

Jesus' wish is to have a relationship with us. Our main purpose is to glorify God and to enjoy him forever.

This means: A life lived for God glorifies him. We strive towards God with our entire being - heart, soul, mind and strength. We abide in Christ and thus act like him, in that we love others. Thereby we bring glory to his name and moreover enjoy the relationship, for which we were originally created.

Whoever wishes to live for God, must first seek the Holy Spirit. This means ceasing to turn to the former person inside us. A life for God means giving up ourselves and instead, longing for God's will more than anything. When we get closer to him and learn to know him better, his wishes will naturally become ours. As we ripen, our wish to obey God's commandments become stronger, because our love for him grows stronger as well.

As Jesus said:
"If you love me, keep my commandments."
John 14,15

Jesus – more than merely a role model

In the first part of this book, you are told how Jesus, the Son of God, brought us the Lord's Prayer. It serves a life turned toward God. Sin lives within us and the spirit of this prayer drives sin out of the soul.

When spiritual healing occurs, converting the low-lying into the exalted, Jesus the Christ is the spirit of transformation. He flows into our hearts as living light. When it begins to glow, it penetrates – little by little – all the spiritual cells, which form the soul, and transmits this light into the physical body.

We are then saturated with the spirit of God, which expresses itself in us through Christ. Jesus is therefore our salvation in every sense of the word. Through our relationship with him and the spreading of his spirit throughout the entire physical body, he introduces us into the mystical spiritual body. Our actual spiritual being is pulled down; and at the same time, our physical bodies are raised and enter into the fiery love of God.

The actual way of every human being

Everything written here concerns every inspired human being. It concerns all of us and helps us to understand, as well as to feel what God had in mind when he created us exactly so.

Not one of us - in the basis of our existence - is better or worse than the other.

Every person implemented the separation solely by means of adopting his/her own conception of life. At birth, all of us grope in the dark spiritually. We are helpless and consciously know nothing. Nonetheless, we feel - unfiltered - all that is around us.

"Where do I come from; I don't know.
Where am I going; I don't know.
What am I here to do; I don't know."

© Manfred Schroeder (*1938, died 21.07.2015),
German-Finnish poet, aphorist and satirist.

The above-mentioned quotation clearly illustrates the spiritual state in which we find ourselves; as well as our actual purpose here. It is not about simply letting our bodies grow, but rather how our entire being should mature. Thereby the goal is to spiritualise our lives and develop into the spirit of God.

If I claim in these lines that this is the only true way to recognise OUR NATURE, there is only one reason for this. My own perceptions go far beyond the traditional comprehension of human senses. Through the spirit of God, which expresses itself fervently within me, I am able to gauge the experiences of the spirit, soul and body individually and in connection to each other. In this way, the sufferings of the soul are well-known to me. I am also aware of the great assignment of the soul, which God appointed it: namely, to be a mediator between spirit and the material, in order that the baseness of the spirit be elevated back into the high presence of God.

Man carries the fall from grace and lives in an overshadowed world, in which the spirit of God is not lived; which is to say, the true and just loving order is absent. To this end, the soul renders the body and the blood warm and vibrant; thereby invigorating the spiritually deficient body. However, if the soul cannot experience the presence of God, its spiritual state deteriorates and it resembles the sluggish human spirit more and more. Thus, body and soul suffer together. The soul is closely intertwined with the body, yet possesses its own independent character. Therefore it can at night – through prayer or meditation – hover as a double beside, in front of, behind, above or below the body. The shape of the soul is similar to that of the body.

Science strives to research the independent life of the soul and possesses no proof of its true existence to this very day. It was claimed for a long time, and still is by some people, that when the body dies, so, too, does the soul and all is obliterated.

This is not so; although the godless person can actually transform the soul into a deathlike state, in which it is forced to experience so-called "hell". However, the strongest and most superior "body" of the "three-body-human" is the spirit. It must be clearly stated here, that words cannot describe this "essence-body".

Spirit is not tangible – it is in a sense akin to air, if a comparison is at all possible at this point. The mind is much denser than the human spirit. Only through internal revelation can lowly man gain access to this higher body. For this we need the sentient body of the soul.

So this means for all of us:

If the inner being, which lives in our physical bodies and is led by the mind, does not depart and give its consciousness over to the soul, we can never attain spiritual knowledge through God.

When we speak of our highest – or higher – self, we mean this spirit-body, which we all strive to experience and know.

The human being in itself feels separated. We try – by means of research, science, experience and power of thought – to recognise more of ourselves and thus silence the inner longing and emptiness. This is how we go through the cycle of living and dying, in order to feel ourselves as whole.

In truth, body, soul and spirit are three different, living beings. Each possesses its own possibility of expressing itself. This is comparable with earth (body), water (soul) and air (spirit).

When the earthly body - the visible person without God - tries to live exclusively as its own identity, the other two being-bodies - the soul and the spirit - will impoverish. The person will become a being consisting purely of intellect.

The goal of earthly life is, however, unity - the joining together of all three bodies. This unification becomes possible through living faith. Nothing else can summon this.

When God expresses himself through people

God mystifies Man

By mysticism, people understand different phenomena. However, inexplicable and incomprehensible things are in most interpretations the same type of classification used to describe mysticism. We endeavour in our outer, perceptible world to understand occurrences which we encounter.

This is our nature. It began through the fall from grace, which Eva instigated in the Garden of Eden, when she accepted the fruit of knowledge of Good and Evil from the serpent and thus became a person of intellect, rather than spirit.

What we cannot grasp, makes us either curious, timid, or fascinates us. Particularly in recent times, we research unknown phenomena, such as ghosts and the like, in order to be able to explain them scientifically.

God is probably the biggest mystery for Man. He is the creator and designer of all life. His being is - and will probably remain - undiscoverable through science.

But what is mysticism or what is a mystic?

We can become many things. We learn various professions and - at the best - we develop into that, which satisfies our hearts' desires, or we recognise our inner calling. When the latter happens, we encounter the essence of mysticism. The invisible inside us begins to show itself and ignites a so-called "fire" within us. It flares up in its revealed gift, which wants to express itself. Such individuals are wholly and completely inspired by their professions, because these come from the invisible into the minds of the external, materially living human beings.

This is a mystical experience. It happens quite often to visual artists, musicians and all creative or people in helping professions, such as physicians or naturopaths.

When we delve deeply into the essence of mysticism, however, we become extremely humble, because in this area we also encounter the essence of God.

During the Middle Ages, mysticism was equated with dark, diabolical and excruciating experiences. Witches were burned at the stake for it, rituals were performed, and the persecution of heresy took place on a daily basis. This facet of mysticism, however, comes from a different source. God's adversary lures the unsuspecting individual into false strength and in this manner draws spiritual strength away form the soul. This process is called soul-catching and is practised up to the present day. We can recognise this mystical experience in members of the New Age movement, for example.

The serious truth seeker, however, sees through this process and recognises its intrinsic great danger. He/she knows that the devil's hand is in this.

The true essence of mysticism is growing into the spirit of God, empathising with his being and thereby living life together with him. Experiencing this has nothing in common with the above mentioned mystical experiences of the Middle Ages or those of the New Age movement.

Here man penetrates into the essence of God, through his call and his attracting the human spirit. This is more than unusual, for humans belong to the Earth and the spiritual strength is nowhere near comparable to the strength which the mystic - or rather, the individual who is becoming a mystic - experiences, when God approaches him/her so closely, that he/she bathes in the Lord's spirit-fire.

Man is the lower being, God is the Highest. Thus an extraordinary spiritual energy encounters human nature and the powers of mystical experience pervade this person. He/she enters into the world of God, where every feeling is of indescribable character. When we speak of love and peace, bliss, joy and other positive emotions, these are mere words compared to what is revealed to the mystic in the home of God. He/she experiences stages of spiritual encounter all the way up to unity with God. No-one can experience anything like this on Earth, if God is not involved.

Solely God can make this possible

Nearly all mystics on their way to God must endure various pains and extraordinary stages of suffering. They will be permeated by the essence of God. Their bodies, however, remain subject to the natural laws of the earthly realm - mortality and deterioration. Thus, the human body is an imperfect vessel for the continuous energy waves of God. The individual therefore reacts with the symptoms of dying and the shedding of the soul; but never fully until death, only to the extent of the brink of death. By the same token, the spirit of the mystic is permeated with the spirit of God; which is inspirational and without boundaries. The mortal human and the soul, however, reside in the material world. Thus the mystic undergoes the "Dark Night of the Soul". God's spirit shines brightly and clearly within it, but the earthly vessel is too dense and cannot absorb this radiance. Thus the earthly vessel seems to be dark and far removed from God.

For people who live intentionally without God, this distance from him is a permanent spiritual condition. Their souls suffer indescribably intensely under the loss of not being able to receive God - and their spiritual condition is nearly wretched. All the suffering of mankind is based on this. If the soul cannot experience itself in God's presence, it faces suffering; and this acts upon it and draws it away from the sacred path of love and spiritual peace. This unfortunate individual is desperately trying to turn his/her life around, to overcome every type of suffering, and still does not understand that only through the Holy Spirit, through the spirit of God, can he/she mature from the Low to the High. Thus will he/she continue to seek and be forced to live as an empty shell, unless he/she turns to God - and does so without compromise.

If we decide to live life based on the Lord's Prayer, we will gradually develop into people who become more and more like Christ.

"I have been crucified with Christ and I no longer live, but Christ lives in me. The life I now live in the body, I live by faith in the Son of God, who loved me and gave himself for me."

Galatians 2,20

Jesus heals the character of man that has been formed by his intellect and he frees the "heart of stone" within us. When this happens, God comes. We then break through all the walls of this world into the nearness of God. Our entire being; body, soul and mind are now touched by his love.

The path of spiritual development

All three bodies of human existence carry different tasks within themselves on the path to spiritual development. Their spiritual essence, which is given by God, produces these differences. Describing these forms of being; of existence, correctly, is truly impossible.

In truth, our consciousness actually rests upon and in the soul. It is the mediator between these two essences of being: that of the body and that of the human spirit.

It is capable of choosing which spirit it wishes to hear. It experiences both the inner and outer worlds, and takes part equally in both of them.

The spirit, on the other hand, contains the conscience within itself. It is the mediator between God and the soul-body. The will of God penetrates through this spirit and one could describe it as divided into two parts. It carries within itself a part, which has not fallen - that which did not become lost in sin - and a spirit in the process of falling.

Although it carries the conscience of God in it, the spirit is by no means equal to God. But it has the responsibility of becoming divine and of being like God.

Every spirit stems from the realm of God, before it is given to its body-soul. All of them stem from the original source of God and were absolutely pure at the hour of their birth. However, they were not able to hold onto this unity and became woven into the Luciferian forces. This spiritual fall happened of their own accord. They lost their inner humility and therefore gave up the obedience to carry out the will of God; thereby giving sway to their own will.

God, however, did not give up on these spirits. He allowed the world of contradictions to emerge and he sent the spirits into this world, to which they felt themselves attracted. Every soul was given its fitting body and the awareness of being able to turn to the Good. The soul, however is influenced by the fallen spirit - and for this reason, man chose to develop questionable moral fibre.

Thus, the sinful human was born.

His purpose, however, was to hear the conscience of God, which penetrates into the consciousness of the soul, so that it may once again renew the divine essence within man. For even in the deeply fallen spirits, the spark of God's love, the Christ spark, exists in the heart of the human and soul body. The contradictions to which the spirit is exposed on Earth do not serve the spiritual development out of arbitrariness. They did not arise by chance and must not be attributed to Lucifer or Adam and Eve alone.

God's creatures are to enter into God-childhood freely - and without coercion - and make purity possible for themselves.

Thus, God had to let good and evil happen, so that mankind might - in the experience of opposites - return to the consciousness of divinity, to the will and obedience of God. This was not a punishment from God, but rather the loving heart of a father who gave his children the highest experience of maturity. This may also be the answer to the questions of some of us, as to why God allows all this to happen to us on this earth; in this world.

Expansion of consciousness and spiritualisation are thus a deliberate process of development in which the spirit comes out of the spiritual realm into the earthly world and thus into the confines of a solid body. It becomes coarse and abandons spiritual refinement in order to burst open the doors and limitations of this prison and return to spiritual freedom.

On Earth as it is in Heaven.

So the human spirit is allowed to bring God to earth. Even the lowest spirit possesses this gift of God to rise up through the consciousness of its soul. It is - like the body - its earthly garment, which enables it to learn to know earthly life by means of the senses given to it. It is so far removed from the presence of God that it completely forgot where it came from and for what purpose.

To clarify it here once again:

God created man so perfect, that he alone can decide for himself which path to take. He can choose heaven, the spiritually pure, or the earthly, the animal, the sensual. The soul has a life of its own, which many people are not even aware of. It can decide whether it chooses the lower or the higher. But the outer human being, with his/her tools, senses and intellect, with emotionality and mentality, has a strong influence on this decision.

If the soul is strongly influenced by the actions of the person, then the spirit, which establishes the conscience of God, cannot penetrate earthly existence. Thus the soul remains trapped in the earthy realm and possesses only a slight conscience.

Thus, the soul is influenced by a person's comportment; and said comportment influences the spirit, as well. If we - as mortal humans - do a lot of good, our souls will be kind. A kind soul can perceive the advice of God and can thereby steer its consciousness towards the Higher, inwardly, into the spiritual region.

The path of spirituality begins with mankind's positive thoughts, words and deeds.

If we pray often and - above all - decide to begin a relationship with God, then the soul relinquishes its dual work and pours it out into our essence, thereby producing various symptoms in us. Its desire is to drive out evil, so that it can empower the spirit, which gives itself over to the consciousness of God more and more. We become purified.

If the Lord's Prayer is prayed - and lived - it brings the spirit, soul and body to God-childhood and we grow into heaven.

Therefore let us pray together ...

Our Father, who art in Heaven,
Hallowed be thy name.
Thy kingdom come.
Thy will be done, on Earth as it is in Heaven.
Give us today our daily bread;
And forgive us our trespasses,
As we forgive those who trespass against us;
And lead us not into temptation,
But deliver us from evil.
For thine is the kingdom and the power
And the glory, forever and ever.
AMEN.

Epilogue

Now you can pray.

The highest form of prayer occurs when thoughts and the thinker become one. He/she is the mystic and becomes the prayer.

The important structure of a prayer is the affirmative form – YES, I believe that your kingdom is coming – yes, thy kingdom come. The inner, positive attitude is important for the development of the soul. It affirms God in its very being and thus, the prayer frees the soul from the prison of earthly existence. Principally speaking, your heart decides how you pray. If it is attuned to God, your nature and your word will always be correct.

Be constantly blessed!

About the authoress

Andrea Regina Kathatrina InEssenz is an original Christian mystic of contemporary times. She lives a mystical life and helps people to find access to God once again. This occurs by means of the spiritual fire of love, which operates through Andrea as a beneficial power for mankind.

Andrea's healing is - through her deep connection to Jesus Christ - primarily Christian and essential.

A true sage will show you time and time again where you are still unaware.

A true leader is concerned with your shadows; for they are the causes of your suffering. They have fallen away from love and grope around in darkness.

The sage illuminates what is essential for them. Consequently, the journey home begins for the soul. Light of light ... So be it!

Encounters with Andrea Regina Katharina

The great love of God flows through Andrea's body into the outside world and thereby helps all beings; human and animal alike; to attain personal transformation. The proximity of God is the vehicle which through the presence - the pure being of Andrea - is given.

The path to annexation into human nature placed a veil over free, spiritual strength and caused forgetfulness of that which is TRUE. Thereby a new spiritual world arose - the visible world, which everyman perceives and helps to shape. This is, however, merely a copy of the impermeable spirit and needs to be cleansed, clarified and to return to the pure source. This is the longing of mankind.

Andrea's great mission is to let us experience our own light again. This happens through Christ and God Himself, both of whom manifest themselves through the mere presence of Andrea. Her existence here on Earth is an act of grace and a gift to all humanity.

The only wish
Andrea Regina Katharina InEssenz has is:

“May a healthy spiritual attitude and intense love of God be given to all people. It is quite easy to love God, as he demands nothing ... He only wishes to be loved.“

You can find contact, videos and the possibility of an encounter with Andrea Regina Katharina InEssenz on her website:
www.andrea-inessenz.de

Table of Contents

Previous books by Andrea InEssenz:

Many people search for the Royal Road in their lives. Numerous spiritual propositions - especially those of esoteric or shamanistic nature - claim to be able to offer the seeker a way of experiencing redemption or liberation. Is that the true Royal Road? How does one find it? In recent times the search for redemption has reached the collective human consciousness. Countless people are already underway to discover it. They have created many rituals, relics and writings in order to glimpse a spark of truth and light.

When all veils fall, faith can be experienced and becomes the only certainty. Here rests quintessential liberation and peace. Thus a person will be redeemed. The only true Royal Road is the path to our Creator, to God. His son Jesus Christ walked this path, as did other individuals thereafter.

This work is for all people: the unbelievers, churchgoers, and all spiritual seekers and practitioners. These writings will perhaps awaken or provoke outrage. Only the person who has opened a spark of truth within him-/herself, will - as though intoxicated - grasp the messages and use them for the good. For them these writings will be a shining light. Receiving the Father of all Creation into oneself and letting His presence mature into the truth is significantly more important than exalted feelings or the knowledge, which humanity so highly values.

Royal Road - Where are you? (Paperback) € 8,-
ISBN 978-3949324-01-7 (February 2021 / 108 pages)

The Child-Father relationship to God is a natural state inherent in the spirit and soul of every human being.

Through the mystical path of the authoress - which was so deeply moved by God's spiritual fire, that all separation between her and God was removed - she explains in wisdom the true path of every soul. Her method of expression shows that she is one with God and bears no dogmas.

This book contains the truth about human development and frees the reader from errors and erroneous conditioning. By means of the mystic's perception as elucidated in this book, the reader can enter the level of true existence: the soul, which carries eternal life. Profound insights and veracity are the gifts of this work, which was written in the name of God.

Thus the reader can build a new relationship with him-/herself, with his or her soul and with God - as well as recognising that Christ is the way to peace.

The True Life of the Soul (Paperback) € 16,-

ISBN 978-3949324-06-2 (May 2021 / 192 pages)

All these books by the authoress are available in bookstores, by amazon in many countries or at edition inessenz: **www.andrea-inessenz.de**

This writing is meant to enhance cognisance. There is but one truth to be recognised: We are children of God and carry within us the power - which was given us by Him - to reveal the errors of this world and to overcome them.

There is only one path to this end:
„I am the way, the truth and the life."
Jesus, the Christ

People call themselves awakened; and whoever is truly awakened will be renewed in Christ. Read these living words and be refreshed through the Holy Spirit.
„Only when the soul is in heavenly order and the seven spirits of God are working within it, is it possible to experience spirituality. Until this time will the soul be snared within the seven spirits of the world."
This world has been seduced by dark forces. What these are, you will find in the contents of this book
Whoever can allow themselves to absorb the message, will awaken from a long sleep. The spirit needs living nourishment! The time for it is NOW.
This book can be the key you have always sought.
That is the purpose of your life - that is why you are a human being! May peace be with you.

The 7 World-Demons

and Salvation through Jesus, The CHRIST

Paperback — Oct 2021 / 80 pages

ISBN 978-3949324-07-9 € 9,52

Walk with Jesus

Mankind returns to God

This book supports you in recognising the necessity of giving your life over to Jesus.

Without Jesus, healing is not possible on any level; and your own knowledge applies only to this world. Walking with Jesus opens your mind and your heart.

Be full of joy and protected in his presence.
So be it ...

ISBN 978-3949324-08-6 (PB) Nov 21 / 40 pages € 5,55

The Spiritual Condition of the World

This book gives you true consciousness. God is all for which you should strive.

He should be the natural state of your spirit. You should become flesh brought to life. Alive as an eternal being.

Go with Jesus, and your search ends. May you all be embraced and feel infinite love.

ISBN 978-3949324-10-9 (PB) Nov 21 / 44 pages € 5,55

www.ingramcontent.com/pod-product-compliance
Lightning Source LLC
LaVergne TN
LVHW010118170826
845678LV00012B/2469

* 9 7 8 3 9 4 9 3 2 4 1 7 8 *